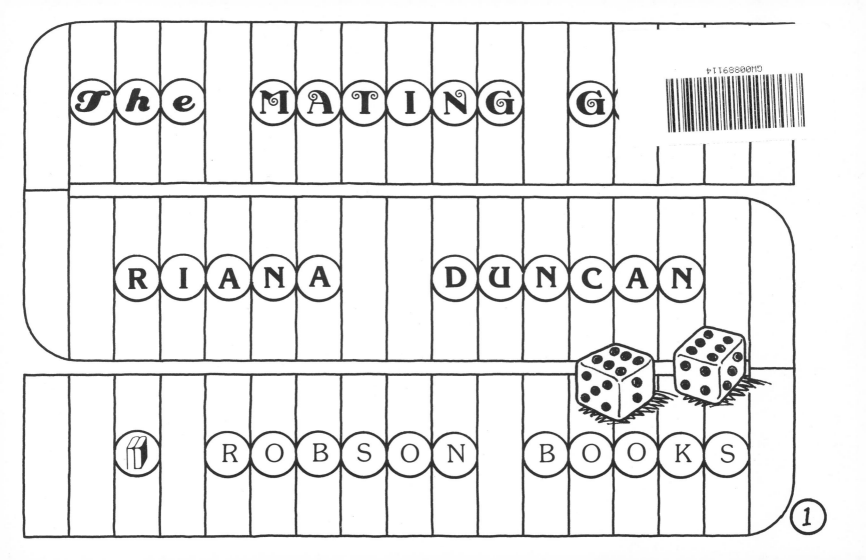

For Andy and Candy Keen

First published in Great Britain in 1988 by Robson Books Ltd,
Bolsover House, 5–6 Clipstone Street, London W1P 7EB.

Copyright © 1988 Riana Duncan

**British Library Cataloguing in Publication Data**

Duncan, Riana
  The mating game : free fun game under the
  cover
  I. Title
  741.5'942
ISBN 0–86051–534–6

Printed in Great Britain by St Edmundsbury Press Ltd, Bury
St Edmunds, Suffolk

Bound by Dorstel Press Ltd, Harlow, Essex

# How to play the game

THE MATING GAME is a bit like poker, in that bluff plays a very large part. All similarity ends there, however, as calling the other's bluff invariably sees one out of the game.

The game is usually played by two people, although there are no hard rules about this. Players have been known to change partners halfway through or string several along at a time. Cheating is an accepted part.

Whatever the number of participants, the principal purpose of the game is to finish it.

The game, at this stage, is played by throwing a pair of dice. The ashtrays and frying pans follow later and really belong to a different game.

The board is divided into red, pink and yellow spaces. The reds and pinks, male and female respectively, are numbered and correspond to the pages in the book. Yellow is neutral.

Whoever scores highest on the first throw starts the game. The number thrown up by the dice each time determines the number of spaces a player moves forward.

When a male lands on a red space he must follow the instructions set out on the page of that number. The same applies to a female who lands on a pink space.

If a male occupies a pink space intended for a female, it's about par for the course. Nothing happens and he stays where he is, unless that space was already occupied by a female and he has landed on top of her. He is then jumping the gun and must sit out a turn.

Should a female settle on a red space meant for a male, she goes neither forward nor back while an uneasy truce is maintained. But she's pushing her luck and can expect him to clear off before the end of the game. If she lands on a red space on top of a male, she has struck a blow for liberation so that's all right. Unless she does it twice running in which case she is a brazen hussy and forfeits two turns.

If either player finishes up on a yellow space, even if that space is already taken, he or she can enjoy a much-needed rest and stay there until the next turn. It's an exhausting business, the Mating Game.

He says, haven't we met somewhere before? He says, what's a nice girl like
you doing in a place like this? He says, where have you been all my life?
*Back to start to bone up on the poets. Try again when you have some better lines.*

He lies through his teeth and says he doesn't respect a girl who does it the first time.

*Move 3 places closer to the second time.*

5

She says she may be old-fashioned but she believes a woman's role to be
that of homemaker.

*You move up 4 places in less than it takes to flick a duster.*

He says he may be old-fashioned but he believes a woman's role to be that of homemaker.

*Miss a turn and wash your mouth.*

She gives him her telephone number.

*Advance 1*

She gives EVERYONE her telephone number.

*Stay where you are.*

9 ♀

She shows a bit of flesh.

*You gain 2 places.*

He shows a bit of flesh.

*Take up jogging and run back 3 places. No liquid refreshments.*

She gives him TWO biscuits with his coffee.

*Advance 4 places.*

12

He pays her a compliment for the way she's dressed.

*As a penalty for sexual harassment, sit out a turn and stir your own coffee.*

She says she is the boss's daughter.

*Move up 5 places.*

He says Robert Redford is a close personal friend.

*Move up 4.*

He offers her a light.

*Advance 2 places.*

(16)

She overdid the lot, but particularly the lashes.

*Stay where you are.*

He takes her to a concert.

*Move up 1.*

He falls asleep.

*Going back 11 places should wake you up.*

She lets him do the choosing and says she'll have whatever he's having.

*You earn yourself 2 places by leaving assertiveness to him and the wine.*

He lets her do the choosing and says he'll have whatever she's having.

*You lose 3 places for letting the wine be more assertive than you.*

He tells her that he reads Proust.

*Advance 1 place.*

She tells him that she reads.

*Go back 3 places, unless you read cookery books in which case advance 4.*

He says he doesn't want any ties as yet.

*Miss 2 turns or say you didn't mean it and surprise her with a quart of French perfume.*

She says she doesn't want any ties as yet.

*You are 2 places nearer to scoring.*

He offers her a lift home and, halfway there, stops the car in a quiet spot.

*Stay where you are. You were going to, anyway.*

Because he's out of petrol.

*Miss 2 turns.*

He says he values friendship more than sex.

*You gain 6 places.*

She says she values friendship more than sex.

*Drop back 5 places.*

29

He says he's never had much dress sense. What he needs is a woman's touch.

*You've hit the right note exactly and move up 3 places.*

She makes fun of his lack of dress sense and says what he needs is a woman's touch.

*You drop back 3 places, without even the chance to choose his tie.*

31

He shows her his Porsche and has practically scored.

*Advance 17 places.*

32

He shows her the repossession papers on his Porsche.

*You are right back where you started, with NO insider dealing on the way.*

He says of course her dog isn't being a nuisance, he loves animals.

*Move up 3 places.*

She says of course his cat isn't being a nuisance, she loves animals.

*Move up 2 places.*

She shows an interest in his hobby.

*Advance 1 place.*

36

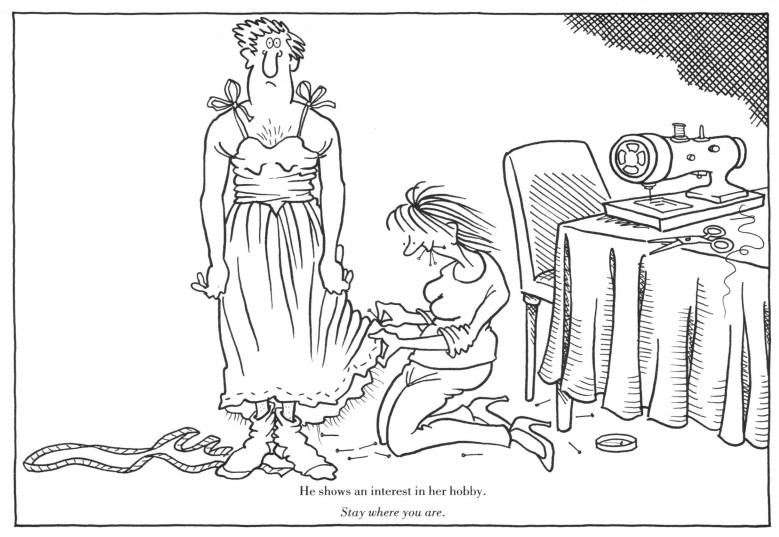

He shows an interest in her hobby.

*Stay where you are.*

He blows a week's wages on taking her to a five-star restaurant.

*Your sacrifice impresses but only earns you a word with your bank manager. Stay where you are.*

She is on a diet because she thinks he prefers slim girls.

*Miss a turn and chase the lettuce leaf around the plate.*

He recognizes her scent.

*Move up 3 places.*

40

His ex used to wear it.

*Go back 6 places, while reflecting on tact.*

(41)

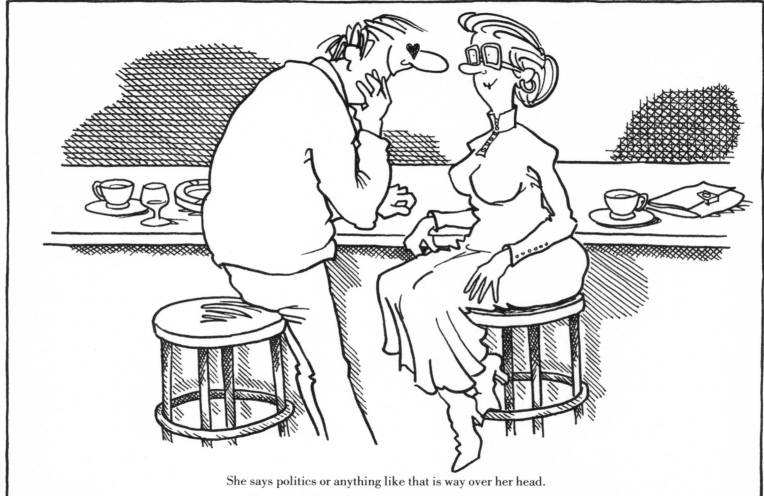

She says politics or anything like that is way over her head.

*Move up 3 places for acting smart by playing dumb.*

42

She confesses she has a degree in political science and modern history.

*Back 5 places, dummy.*

He tells her about his plans for the future.

*You gain 6 places.*

44

She tells him about her plans for the future.

*Back, back, BACK 16 places.*

He says he knows a nice quiet little place just around the corner, where they can be alone.

*Advance 4 places.*

His flat.

*Drop back 5 places for being economical with the truth.*

47

She invites him round for a meal.

*You are 7 places nearer his heart.*

48

She cooks the one thing he can't stand.

*Go back 4 places.*

49

He tells her about his wife.

*You are ahead by 7 places.*

50

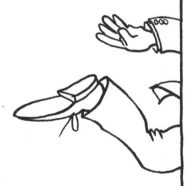

She tells him about her mother.

*You drop out of the game.*

51

He is unwell and looks it.

*You gain immediate sympathy and 2 places.*

She is unwell and looks it.

*Go back 5 places where he can't see you.*

He badly miscalculates the value of a meal plus double brandies after.

*Miss a turn and have an early night.*

54

He makes up for his error by treating her to a holiday in the Seychelles and loses her to the bronzed beefcake loafing outside the arrival lounge.

*Go back and take up stamp collecting instead.*

She writes off her car and says never mind, Daddy will replace it.
*You advance 11 places in 0.016 seconds.*

He writes off his car and says damn, he hadn't even finished paying it off yet.

*You drop back 5 places faster than the speed of light.*

He tells her about his promotion.

*As an added perk, move up 3 places.*

She tells him about her promotion.

*Miss 2 turns and he might come back.*

He takes her to a disco to dance the night away.

*Move up 4 places.*

60

He puts his back out.

*Miss 3 turns or start again with someone your own age.*

61 ♂

She beats him at squash.

*You have disregarded one of the most fundamental rules of the mating game.*
*Drop back 5 places.*

She lets him beat her at squash.

*Game, set and match to you. Move up 6 places.*

He says he doesn't suppose she's old enough to remember the Beatles.

*You gain 1 place for flattery. If you were serious, miss a turn and see an optician.*

64

She gives her age away and says she can remember when men were men.

*Drag yourself back 8 places.*

She knits him a sweater.

*You gain 3 places for effort but lose 6 for execution.*

He wears it.

*You move 4 places nearer being able to take it off again.*

He fixes the thingy on her car and he's well away.

*Move up 3 places.*

She fixes the thingy on his car and he's well away.

Miss a turn and learn to knit, cook and sew.

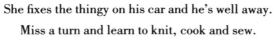

He gives her a nice bottle of perfume.
*You move up a place in her affection.*

He says it was duty-free.
*You pay for it by going back 6 places.*

He is nice to her mother. This makes her like him.

*Crawl on and gain 2 places.*

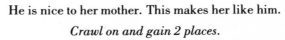

(72)

She is nice to his mother. This makes her suspicious.

*You might as well drop back 3 places, because Mummy will insist that you do.*

He is honest.

*Honestly . . . . Go back 5 places.*

74

He lies.

*You gain 4 places.*

75

She invites him up for a nightcap.

*You are 3 places nearer the finish.*

76

He misinterprets the rules of the game.

*Miss a go and get dressed.*

77

He says beauty doesn't impress him, he prefers a girl with a bit of character in her face.

*Miss a turn and practise the following: God, you really are the most beautiful thing ever to walk into my life, where did you get those amazing eyes?*

She says love has liberated her, she's giving up the contact lenses, the false
eyelashes, the padded bras. What you see is what you get.

*You fool, he WANTED to be fooled. Go back 12 places.*

She overdoes the drinkies.

*He'll see to it that you move up 8 places.*

He overdoes the drinkies.

*Sleep it off till the next game.*

81 ♂

She tells him she's a virgin.

*Advance 6 places. If you lied, miss a turn.*

He confesses he's a virgin.

*Miss 2 turns and use the time to get some practice.*

She forgot to tell him about the kids.

*Remember to go back 9 places.*

He forgot to tell her about the alimony payments to the two ex-wives.

*Your amnesia costs you 10 places, but not the bill for night-club drinks.*

He carves her name and his, for posterity.

*You're 1 place nearer your goal.*

Wrong girl, wrong name.

*Shakespeare was wrong. Forget about a rose by any other name, just go back 13 places.*

87

She displays a sense of humour at the absurdity of it all.

*You've convinced him women don't know a joke when they see one. Back 7 places.*

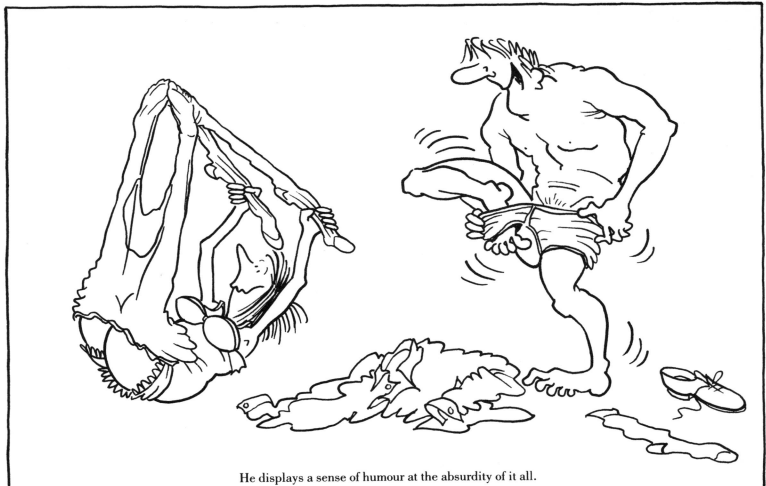

He displays a sense of humour at the absurdity of it all.

*If you can manage to disentangle yourself, move up 1 place.*

He says he's not much of a one to put his feelings into words and if she thinks he'll make a nerd of himself by saying 'I love you', she can think again.

*Go back 5 places.*

So would she please accept this gold bracelet instead?

*By letting your wallet talk louder than words you gain 6 places.*

91

She says she is tired of waiting, they are both adults after all, there are plenty of other men in the world.

*Go back to start and find one.*

He says he is tired of waiting, they are both adults after all, there are plenty of other women in the world.

*You've scored. Go straight to finish.*

She says she can't live without him, she'll kill herself if he ever leaves her.

*Miss 2 turns and calm down.*

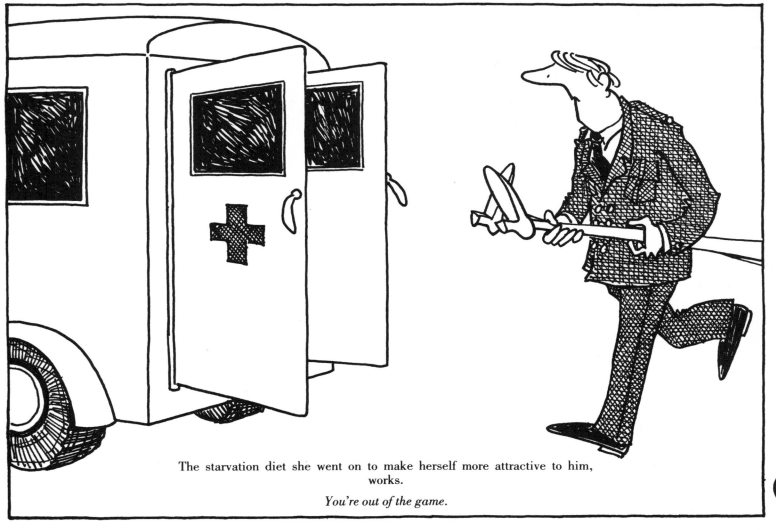

The starvation diet she went on to make herself more attractive to him, works.

*You're out of the game.*

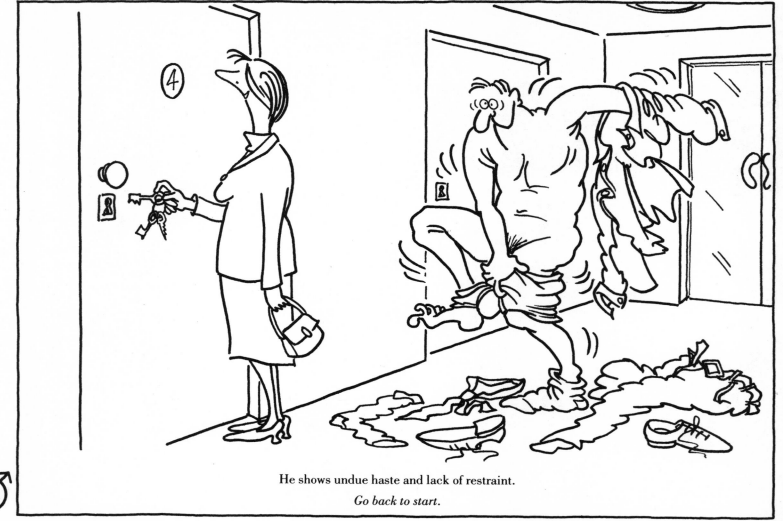

He shows undue haste and lack of restraint.

*Go back to start.*